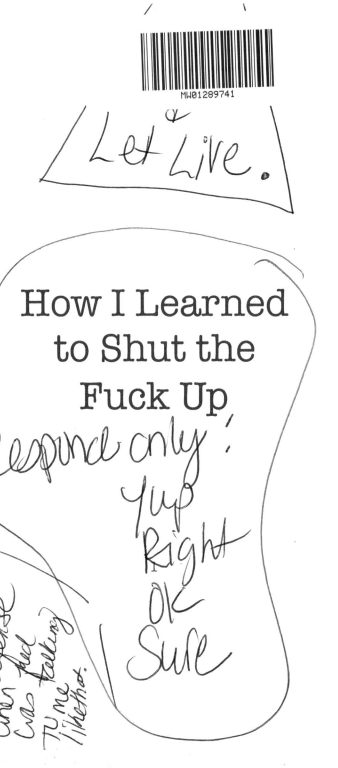

Let Live.

MW01289741

How I Learned to Shut the Fuck Up

Respond only:
Yup
Right
OK
Sure

How I Learned to Shut the Fuck Up

How I Learned to Shut the Fuck Up

By: Armand Cook

Thursday, November 1, 2018
11:40 PM

ArmandCook.com
PostalMontage.com
HowILearnedToShutTheFuckUp.com

How I Learned to Shut the Fuck Up

I chose

I choose

Peace

Preface
It's good to shut ones mouth and
listen- truly listen.
Listen to God.
Yourself.
Also that which someone is saying- I
am not stating that you must do as
they state yet with reason listen and
decide if that which they are stating
is conducive for your life.
For all know something new- even in
ways of observing their mannerisms-
Lessons on that which to do, not to
do, also view a bit- then place your on
spin on it.
It is this- not everyone will nor do
they have to love or accept you.
For-
In a interconnected world- there are
so many facets to the inner world of
the multitude
of humans each of us

will have to come in contact with
during our life time.
Instead of trying to be accepted and
or trying to persuade or convince
others why you should be loved- one
should know x understand their self
worth.
Having self love x self confidence-
coming to terms that not everyone
will love nor accept you.
Though that is more than fine- for
there are many that will cherish you
for that which you are and that
which you are morphing to become.
A piece written on and about the
human condition [Anthropology x
Psychology] - that which one may
face or do and how to have peace in
the mist of it all or personal
acknowledgment- that

said individual can up root.
Knowing that they a capable of
doing all which they desire- while
honoring the life x rights of all and
a reminder or telling they have a
choice in all facets of life-[Health,
Wealth, Love, Happiness] internal
and out.
A reflection
An acknowledgment that no life
isn't a fairytale yet that one's life
x the life of humanity can be made
better- yet it starts one person at a
time x in daily civil human to
human interaction.
-Armand Cook

Acknowledgments

To life- my friend x the greatest
gift that I have ever known.
You have been with me from my
conception and will be there with
me in the end.
My friend- it is exciting to know
that as the moments ever flow, to
you x I, this is only the beginning!
I appreciate you exceedingly so-
gratitude for allowing me to dwell
in this realm.
To God- my friend, gratitude to
you for the gift above and all that
you have freely

place x given within it.
Choice, Health, Family x Loved
Ones, Gifts x Talents, the capacity
to learn x do all that I desire.
You are more than my friend you
are my supply and I appreciate
you doing that which you do-
simply because it pleases you.
Together my friend- this is only
the beginning!
Lastly- to the days composing this
writing and also to my mind
conceiving new things on the
daily.
I Thank Myself x Loved Ones for
Everything!

Introduction

How I Learned to Shut the Fuck Up

Armand Cook

Paradox

Paradoxical

Understood that this can sound paradoxical yet understand that most all things have two sides or is multifaceted-
Having another side to the coin, blade, story, view etc- that goes for our fellow humans.

This is not a cynical writing-
more as a view into everyday
phenomena of psychology x
anthropology.
Human to human interaction x
communication- social skills.

Understanding x Knowing that
life is not a fairytale yet there
ways to have peace x bliss, etc
in the mist of it all-
living fully x having full
expression of oneself.

In the end-
I do believe x have faith in people.
Our human race.
I believe x know that the concept
of Meliorism
["That through human effort the
world can be made a better place"]
is more than real x possible.
Yet I know that life is not a
fairytale.

I believe that the human mind is
astonishing-
That when people of a like mind
come together, that truly amazing
things come to fruition.

Knowing that there are many that are free in body having the ability to be free in mind- with that being stated, those of us that are x chose or are about to choose to be such a human, have the ability to come together x make that a reality for those that are being bondage in body x mind.

It doesn't matter if two or more a that come to together are in the same career, this or that x doing they same thing, we don't have to-

14

There is beauty in difference
yet being of like mind in the
facet that we are people of
progression.
In all facet of our being.
Knowing that everyday we
can get better and better- in
all facets of life x being.

Out of billions in our ever growing interconnected world- there are more than enough people to communicate with in a civil human to human manner x capacity.

Even if 99.99% of the
planet were not for you,
there are still a number of
people that will enjoy and
love you.
Those that rock with you
x are fond of you- great.
You don't have to always
state your case on why
you should be loved x
accepted.
Do you know that which
beauty is?
Beauty is you.

1.) This is how I learned to stuff the fuck up

Saying all this to say- that there is a time to speak and a time to stay silent.
Response over reaction.
Never allow anyone to control nor dictate your mood x emotions, thoughts, behavior actions.
You are in control of you.
When engaging in communication- make your words count.

Express yourself fully.
That way you may be
understood-
Understand that some will x
some won't yet you have to do
your part to be received x
understood.
Know that not everyone will
understand nor accept you.
Yet that is more than fine- for
there are many that will.
Lastly regardless-
Love Yourself x Know Your
Worth

2 .) Most people desire to live life by a syllabus

—They want to be told what to do, how to do it, when to do it.
—Not viewing life as art- free, open etc.
They would rather have to book written for them to regurgitate, instead visualize it and placing words onto page for others to enjoy x learn from.
Looking for someone to hold their hand,

walking them step
by step for most all matters in
life.
Life is to be experienced and
enjoyed- helping others when
one can- living fully, while
honoring the life x rights of all.
No rubric for how each should
live- understand that iron
sharpens iron and while that
being said, that we can learn
from one another in our
differences.
Yet to depend- no, you have all
that you need within and that
which is outside of oneself-

that is required will arrive in
due time.
It is doing grand things with
that which is freely given to
you.

3.) People have the ability to be Great- [though they already are for they are human] yet at the same time choose the comfort zone over Living Greatness.

—Yes greatness and success is dependent upon oneself x their own perception.
—Yet there comes a time x moment when one has the ability to do more, be more- etc.
—To change the paradigm for their

life- not only their
life but the lives of their family
and humanity.
—I firmly believe in doing that
which one can when they can.
Yet at the same time doing more
when they are able to do more.
It's simple.
It is as a thought, I thought long
ago-
It is this- "I am as a rock being
thrown into water x I am
throwing myself in the the
water constantly- before the
ripples went out as far as they
could. Now they go out further-
as I

progress in my exploration x
experience x development of
life- my ripples will go out
wider and wider."
There is much, much, much
more to the thought indeed
yet-
Success x Greatness is a
choice- yes it is dependent
upon oneself- yet one cannot
do something long ago and
state five, 10, 20 plus years
later that, that thing carries
the same weight- are you still
alive?
If so do more!

There are more mountains to climb, people to help, things to say, things to create- you are alive- use your gifts- cause your ripples to expand!
—If those that you converse with do not desire such things leave them on the top of that one mountain- you go and explore, achieve, experience more life, greatness, success!

some I know

4.) Most people want love yet aren't willing to pay the cost.

—The cost to love—
1.) Vulnerability
2.) Time
3.) Communication
4.) Understanding
5.) Forgiveness x Reconciliation
6.) At times place self interest aside *LMAO!*
7.) Choosing to love day after day x moment to moment.

—Yes of course one can come up with

27

7/27/23

more to place onto the list.
Yet these are the cost to love.
—Some will state that they love
you- yet aren't willing to
express, share, do the things it
take to love.
—Understood that things come
up- indeed yet being able to over
come them together.
If they aren't willing to do such
things- save your words x peace
and move on.
—Yet I must also state that if
one is harming any facets of
you- it would be wise to leave
that situation promptly.
Love Yourself- Gratitude.

28

Be gentle with one another for all exhibit various traits at various times in this thing we know as life.

Be gentle yet diligent, responsible, accountable with yourself.

Love yourself!
No one else matters —

5.) People love you until they hate you x hate you until they love you.

—That being said why waste precious time trying to converse, persuade, convince, prove- anything synonyms to those word with others.
—Whether they clap or boo- love yourself. No cliche- be the best that you can be each day. It's doesn't matter

what they think nor that with they say.
—Know your worth- have peace- and remember to not chase a butterfly- allow it to come freely. When x if it flies away- peace within.

—

6.) The more you say the more people they believe that they know you, yet understand that people only understand x comprehend only up to the level that they are.

31

.

—Most do not allow others to just live life- not understanding that all have but no choice but to show their fruit. Instead of communing and enjoying the moments of the infinite with one another, they would rather try to "figure you out".

—Enjoy the silence x peace of not engaging in experiences with a individual as that.

7.) Most people care about health when it is to late

—They eat this and that
—Drink this and that
—Take the prescription- that which does not cure yet only suppresses the root of the issue- giving one various side effects.
—No thought for the future.

—Not investing in the top
factor of life-
[a body in harmony.]
For without health
neither knowledge nor
wealth taste as delightful.
Health allows one to
provide, protect, help,
defend and the list goes on
for family x humanity.
Quiet yourself- let them
eat x live as they please.

8.) Most people allow money to rule them whether through giving up health, family, peace for the obtainment of it [OR] by not having any and worrying about it.

—Live outside the matrix of it all and simply create multiple streams of income.
There are an ocean of legal ways to earn money.

—Simply apply
application, resilience x
persistent.
Use the tool- money to
change the paradigm of
your life.
By one having the right
relationship with money.
[Money is a tool -Armand
Cook]

9.) People Don't know that Money is a tool. They don't want to invest, save nor care about money [that which money can do] nor the future.

—Security is not a real thing nor is money- [It is yet again it isn't.]
—Though there is a way to have higher chances of security or take care of various things that arise x could arise.
—It is by the concept x piece of cotton and flax, that is cut into a triangle with a Presidents or inventors face on it.
—That is back up by a metal that comes naturally from the ground.

[Money]
Money is a tool
Money is energy
Money- is the thing that greases
the wheel.
—I once had a conversation with
someone that stated that money
can not buy happiness.
I laughed- I stated something
along the lines of "Is that so? Tell
me what does."
They stated "Love"
I rebuttal with"What about those
that take their life- don't they have
loved ones- those that love them
ever so deeply? Yet they still take
their life" (At this point I stated
more yet this is a sound bite). So
we see that it isn't love that buys
happiness.

38

Happiness is dependent upon
oneself- If one is happy because
they desire x chose to be happy
then all things can flow x bring joy
to their life.
For who has ever been annoyed by
being able to feed their family?
Who has been unhappy giving to
the homeless or paying for their
own home?
No one!
There is a order to it all-
My personal order is:
God
Health
Family
Money
Humanity
[Here is another sound bite,
though there is more to it]

—God, for He is my everything, my supply yet most importantly my friend.
—Health for it allows my to provide, protect- etc for myself x my family.
—Family, for family is everything.
—Money for the things that is can do.
It makes it so that one can explore all the facets of life.
[Our PlayGround Earth x Life- For Live Is A PlayGround]
—Humanity for I love the philanthropy x charity- helping others, it is bliss!
—Having God first, it balances everything out for me that is-
Yet has one has to choose happiness- they must also choose God- if they desire to do so.

He brings a grand order to it all.
Money is a tool x the tool of this
playground we call life.
[Lastly- about those taking
their life- that is highly serious
and if you are thinking x feeling
a certain way get help- it is
okay. Also if you know someone
that is struggling- be there for
them x help them obtain help.]

10.) Most people don't want a challenge

—They desire to be spoon feed
as a toddler.
—Crying at the hint of effort
having to be taken.
Challenge is good
Challenge is healthy
It causes those that choose to
face it, to be more than that
which they once were a few
moments ago- it requires a
new x best you.

—Challenge when faced can be conquered in any capacity.
Yet heres the clause*
[It must be faced]
When done one will state, that "it was easier than I thought" and it prepares you x gives to the tools to face that which is next.
Also each time you face anything that is the equivalent or less to the previous challenge, it will seems as a [shoo fly don't bother me x a walk in the park.]

When faced with either
conversing with one that
avoids challenges or not
conversing with them- the
choice is plain to see.
Do not communicate with
those that choose the fetal
position. Stand with those
that stand.

11.) Most people don't know that someone's opinion of them doesn't have to be that which one accepts into their inner world

—Someones opinion of you does not have to be your reality.

—Once had a conversation with two individuals, on two separate occasions and I posed this question-

—"Do you think that you are a nice person?"

I waited to hear-
They replied- "I don't know- I let
x allow others to determine
that."
It came out as if they believed
that response was the
honorable thing to say.
Yet in reality- where is the
power in that?
There is only dependance in
such words, philosophy,
pathway of thinking.
I then stated x inquired further
saying " if 100 people tell you
that you are nice x 100 tells you
are you are mean-
what are you?

46

What are they?
[Confused x Lost]
See where the issue arises?
The answer is that it doesn't
matter.
Their opinion means not a
thing.
You know x God knows- that is
all that matters.
For people can say that you are
nice yet you can be as mean as
they come conversely people
can say that you are mean yet
you can be as pleasant as they
come.
It never mattered that which
they thought x think.

47

All that matters is that you know fully and truly whom you are.

For people can not lie to themselves- yet those that do, kill a piece of themselves that is now lost to oblivion.

You cannot lie to yourself- for while ones alone, the music stops playing, friends go home.

You are stuck with you.

As long as you honor the life x rights of all and live fully- one can rest their head

honestly x peaceful.
It doesn't not remotely
matter that which they
think.
Do not surround yourself
with those that care or give
thought to such things.
For people will think that
which the choose to think.
It is there choice- their God
given right.
Yet it doesn't have to matter
to you what they all
Live free x be free! say!

my life

49

12.) The way someone treats x speaks with another person is the way that you will treat x speak about you.

—They can state many times over "That's x Their or You're Different".
Yet time and time again in most cases that is not the truth.
—For it is as this- no, you may not do the same things as another and yes you are a different

individual- yet what will be
the thing, though different-
that will spawn x breeds the
individual to treat x speak to
you in the same capacity as
they did the other individual?
—Obverse how one treats
Rude ← their family and others.
For you do not want them to
treat the waiter a certain way
and you better- for if you
were the waiter, they would
most likely treat you in the
same capacity.
Converse with one that
desires human to human
civilness with all.

51

13.) Most people are afraid to bring that <u>which is good within</u> them to fruition.

—Why this is?
I have not a clue why one would be afraid to share their talents, gifts, that thing that only they can bring to this planet to fruition.
They are robbing humanity of their light- understood that it is their prerogative x their life.
Yet if they don't, you should- while removing such people from your life.   *Kelsey*

We all know someone that is quite exceptional at one or a multitude of things yet has chosen to sit and do not one thing with it.
<u>Never be as them.</u>
Bring it to fruition- humanity needs it!

–

14.) Most people don't know that strength is love x vulnerability x forgiveness x reconciliation x peace x laughter x etc

—Ever meet a person that thinks because they are mad that they are strong or that makes them right?
It doesn't- could be caused by

something they obverse in their
household or something that
was never checked as a child.
—Most view anger, strife,
pettiness, fighting, no
forgiveness, lack of
vulnerability, telling someone
off and they list goes on as
strength yet that it highly x
truly far from the case.
Love is power.
Strength is love.
Check number 4 for elaboration.

15.) Most people have chosen conformity

—Conformity is death- yet haven't we all conformed in more ways than one?
Yes.
—Yet the capacity on that which I am speaking on, is the way of one not feeling as if they have a choice in the matter.
Thinking that it is a must to live life as one was taught in school, by parents, on television, by

friends and the list goes on.
You have a choice- be free and
know that you can choose and
not only choose, you can
change your mind.
I am not stating to be double
minded.
Far from it-
Be balanced and well in
formed that you truly have a
choice and that you can live
freely x as you desire- as long
as you honor that life and
rights of all.
If you come in contact with
one that states otherwise.
Pay to no mind.

16.) Most people don't understand the power they have- how powerful they are

It is wise to understand your own power.
Freely given power.
1.) Power of Choice
—From that all facets of ones personal powers flow.
Power of Thought
Power Emotion x Feeling
Power of Action
Power of Self Love
Master yourself and you will know bliss x peace.
Knowing that you can be

vulnerability- wearing no mask.
Living Whole x Living Free
We all have choice yet it is in
taming those choices to do that
with you see fit.
Never allowing choices to
control you.
Disciplining them.

–

17.) Happy when- don't
converse with those that are
happy when.

—Happy when the get this
—Happy when they go here
—No
[Happy for no reason.]

Just don't talk about it - just DO NOT!

How I Learned to Shut the Fuck Up

18.) Don't talk about it... don't just talk about it

—Create it! Be it! Do it!
Both have a place yet it is wise
you obverse life, people, oneself
and bring to fruition that which
you delight.

—

19.) Most people don't view that
they are art x that which they
do as art- life as art x business
as art x blank as art- they view
it as another would instead of
how they choose x

59

would like to view it.

—Life for is a blank canvas- for those fortunate enough to be born in an area on Earth that allows you to be free of mind x body this is.

—Life x Business is not a set way, it is out of all that live in the same period of time that you live.

Out of the all- it is a thing of connecting with those that desire to connect with you. Those enjoys your form of art, whether in life or business.

—How do you desire to see it?

Now create x enjoy.

20.) Most people have to see to believe

—This individual has no form of faith- I say that for the reason being, that all can have "faith" on the end result. Whether it is themselves, a home, product, business, endeavor- the list goes on. Seeing is not believing. It is just seeing- Belief is faith. Faith is persistence.

It isn't wise to commune
with one that has no faith
x persistence.
Those are the things that
cause one to stay
steadfast, to obtain x
achieve things- pass that
which they could
conceive.

Just do your best always

21.) Most people fear the unknown

—The unknown is a quite
beautiful place.
We all dwell in it- yet who has
the eyes to see the bliss x
opportunities.
We can plan, plan, plan, plan
and plan some more.
Yet there will always be
unknown variables.
There is no control in the
unknown- other than
acceptance. ⇐

It is by doing ones absolute best
at each endeavor, of any size-
day in and out.

63

Knowing that- by that which
they did today has no choice but
to breed phenomenal results.
It is as planting seeds- you don't
know which will take root and
grow.
Out of the ones that do grow-
there isn't much of a way to
know how many fruit each will
produce.
Nor how many seeds each fruit
will have nor the size of the
fruit.
Yet should you still plant?
Of course x Indeed!
How come?
For that is the only way to reap!

To reap- one must what?
Exactly.
Yet by doing ones best x that which is required, one can enhance their chances in having an abundance of successes.
Uncomforted Zone x Being comfortable while dwelling in the Uncomforted Zone is the realm where possibilities lay freely to the open- yet whom is excited to go?
Those that aren't don't travel with them

22.) Most people despise change

—These are they that you would not find much growth in- other than the fact that they are getting older.
—Change is inevitable
—Change it good
—Change is growth- if one chooses to take hold of the outright yet also hidden beauty x opportunities that change has to offer.
—It can be your greatest friend-

that is if you allow it.
More as a embracement of it.
Those that despise change
wishing things were as they use
to be are stuck x stagnant.
Yes we all have memory and it
can be nice to view the pass-
Yet it is highly dangerous to
view x remain in the pass.
Growth x Change- it's okay.
Yes it may feel a certain way at
times- yet if you allow it- it will
refine you in
grand ways unknown.
-Those that do not want change-
stay away from them.

accept

23.) People feel that they
are entitled.
Stating that they deserve or
that life x someone owes
them something- yet the
truth is that no one owes
anyone anything.

—That is why I state- choose
peace.
When one is kind to you-
have gratitude x
appreciation for they do not
have to be.
Entitlement x the thought
that the world owes one

something is a trait that isn't conducive to ones full expression x growth toward progression in various facet of their life.
Limit communication and allow them live as they desire.

24.) Most people do not enjoy themselves- whether it is- appearance, voice, height, life- etc

—There are a lot of unhappy people
Some a have a legitimate "excuse" x reasons and to them- they are those that I am not speaking on.
Yet the ones that aren't fond of the way their pinky nail grows out of their finger- instead of loving that which they are, fully x truly.

Finding an issue their lives.
If one doesn't enjoy their
life instead of doing that
which is required to make it
into the way they desire for
it to be- they may take it out
on you.
They may blame you
Even get mad when you are
happy.
That is highly toxic-
exceedingly so.
Those are they which I am
describing.

—Don't give company to
their misery

They that don't know nor
understand that they are
the only [them] so with
that being stating- they
are perfect, I am perfect,
you are perfect.
We are perfectly us!

25.) Have to do with number 24- most are going through something and they allow that pain- or that which they would be fond of calling it- to come out upon you.

—It is unfortunate- yet it is a reality that most cope with their pain x that which they would be fond of calling it by placing it upon others.
—Most of the time, on those that

desire to help
them through that which
they are dealing with.
—Never take it personally.
Yet spend no energy, no
words- for until they are
ready to receive, it is as
the conversing with the
grass.

26.) Some people place their limits upon you

—About your aspirations, goals, things [you do]- most have this trait, it is the placement of that which is inside them- upon other. What is within them, they view in others even if that is far from

the case x truth.
Feeling if they cannot,
then other's can't either.
Yes it is exceedingly
narcissist yet it is a
thing that most will face
a few times within their
life time. Yet it is fine-
watch your personal
thoughts- that which
others perceptive,
conceive at times has
nothing to do

76

with you. Lastly it doesn't
have to matter to you- at
all.
—What do you know about
yourself?
—What do you think about
yourself?
—Listen to that- those
beautiful thoughts-
refining your mind, skills,
abilities- all facets of your
self.
—Don't not debate anyone
about that which you are,
your worth- etc.

27.) People say that desire
to be great yet- obverse if
they stick with that which
they desire x start.

—Starters yet never
finishers
—Talkers
—People that take trips to
"Someday Isle".
These are those that have
the same abilities as any
that has ever lived and
done something
that they

desired- yet those who allow [something] to get the way of the obtainment x bring to fruition of that which they personally desire.

These are they- the walking dead.

Allow them to buried themselves as long as the desire- yet do not waste time conversing with them for the is no life where they dwell.

28.) Most say that they desire for you to succeed yet they either don't by any means x ~~don't desire~~ for you to <u>do "better" than</u> ~~them.~~

—They'll cheer- oh yes they'll cheer yet as long as you are where they desire for you to be.
—They give

81

advice x tip to
cause one to be smarter,
more aesthetically please,
stronger, healthy- even
money yet the moment they
see you are on their heels or
past them- they aren't to
fond of that.
—They want you to be their
charity case
Their project
Their thing they tell others
about- stroking their own
egos.
For if you do

dont speak
Let Live

better than them that
makes them uncomfortable
for it shows them a few
things about themselves.
1.) That their pedestal was
fecal matter
2.) That they aren't doing
as much as they can
3.) Along with other things-
the fact they don't want you
to be better than them.
Don't speak- let live.

29.) Most smile in ours face x speak behind ones back

—They justify their personal weakness by the saying "If you don't have anything x nothing nice to say- don't say anything at all"
Hmm- true?
If you so- they have forgotten the end x most important part of the saying.

"Don't say anything at all"
They tell x speak about
you to everyone but you-
they speak for the sake of
their toxic behaviors x
traits- as well as the
others, that will not tell
them to level up and be a
big person within their
inner being by having a
conversation exclusively
with you- the individual
that they are speak

on.
They choose to smile in
ones face yet speak behind
ons back- over the beauty of
reconciliation x
understanding.
They have forgotten the
saying yet you have not-
Say nothing at all to them-
allow them to be.

-Another thought-
People say they won't tell
then

tell
Most all that you know say
something about you or you
tell them something then say
it to another person after
stating that they will never
tell anyone.

—In terms of real secrets or
things that you desire to be
truly concealed- even if the
communication x the
relationship in capacity-
friendship or otherwise goes
to

Say not.

How I Learned to Shut the Fuck Up

south x sour.
—How to keep those secrets
x concealed- the best way is
to reveal x say not a things.
 —Or to obverse how they
are with others-
1.) Are they speaking on
others in a mean way or
uplifting
2.) Two are they only
speaking on public domain
information or information
that the other individual
would want them to be
silent on.

87

People desire something to
talk about x compare- give
them nothing for when they
do- they dilute themselves.
Yes I will now-
communication x
understand is key.
Yes civil kind
communication can be had-
Yet if one or many desire to
have chaos, confusion etc
you do not have to
communicate
with them for them more
than

likely have
solidified within their
head before the
conversation even started
that which they will do.

30.) Most people complain yet don't do that with is required to change their situations

—This is not only exceedingly toxic- it's dangerous, for it not only touches their outer world yet indeed spawns their inner world.
—Not willing to execute necessary

adjustments x changes to ones life, inner world- yet rather the things that takes a toll on ones character.
—Be wise and avoid communication with one that complains x also those that are able to change x help yet choose to do nothing.

31.) Some have victim mentality

—Anything you say or do is an attack to them no matter how kind, practical, loving you come at it- with individuals as that- keep your peace and as we have been learning to do.
Shut you mouth.
—Do not entertain that
*Give no energy to them.

32.) People take things personally

—You can be conversing about how [you] clean your room- and because they are neglectful to do such things, they feel a certain way.
—Yet you may have never been within their domain and was just conversing freely- as you should be able to do.
—In most cases as that- Just shut your mouth, for that has nothing to do with you- that is their personal issue.

33.) Some have deep rooted issues, that have nothing to do with you.

—Life experiences they have faced, may have become hard wired within various facets of whom they are- they haven't faced them nor taken responsibility x accountability for themselves. Do not take it personally, for it has nothing to do with you.

34.) Some have complexes

—Obscure traits that fester, at times they may not even be aware that they have them. At times they can be highly dysfunctional to themselves.

—

35.) No empathy until it happens to them x someone they know.

—Harsh views
—No forgiveness
—Justified in their

nastiness to others- until it happens to them and or maybe someone they know and all that goes directly out of the window.
*If they can be this way to another- they can be this way to you.
Be kind yet ["Arms length"]

—

36.) Most people love lies x hate the truth.

—Tell them a lie and they'll lick your anus
—Tell them the truth and they'll "crucify x stone" you.

37.) Most desire a "Yes Human"

—They want you to agree with every thing they say and do.
—No I am not stating disagree for the sake of disagreeing.
I am saying,
—They think that if one has a different path way of thinking than their own- it is wrong.
—That the individual saying something different isn't for them, when that can be far from the case.

38.) Most say they do not like something that someone else does x stated. Saying that- the person is wrong.

—Yet does the same thing in the same way and or to a lower, higher degree, in the same or in a different way.

—

39.) Most people are priggish

—Self-righteous, narrow-minded
—Looking at another as lower
That is a dangerous x toxic pathway to travel on.
Do not travel with them.

40.) Most people judge you before they even have a conversation with you.

—Height, Weight, Hue of Skin, Attire, Hair Style, Ear Shape, Type of Shoes, If your clothes are ironed or not, Walk, Stance- the list goes on.

—They if judge you without getting to know you understanding on a mental plain- it is more than okay, with one not communicating with them.

—Don't take it personally

—Connect with like mind individuals

41.) People hear ideas then act as if the idea was their own

—These are they that you tell nothing, for they are thieves. Ones that you say I am going to do this yet they are about to preform before you and they say either to you or within their inner world. "Why didn't I think of that- that's a good idea" They brainwash themselves in thinking that it was their idea, for they were in the

conversation with
you or they shamelessly
know that it wasn't their
idea and that it will hurt
you directly x indirectly
yet pass it off as their
own.
Give them none of your
words.

42.) Most people envy you in one way or another

—Never understood this one- at all.
—Yet most size others up x compare their efforts x life to yours.
—Truly, it is a toxic trait x behavior
—If they envy you, it is not in ones best interest to associate with them for a number of reasons
Here are two:
1.) No telling that which they will do.
2.) You do not desire for that which they embody- to be apart of you.

102

43.) People act as if your idea is a bad a idea x then turn around x do it themselves x act as if they were the first to come up with it.

—They will state how it's a bad idea- yet watch how in a moment of time they will [not try] they will pawn it off as if they were the true creator of said idea x concept.
—Do not share your world with individuals as this.

44.) People have a hard time giving credit

—You'll both decide to do a certain endeavor together- yet they'll state words as [I x My]
—I x My people- when it was really a collaboration of two or a team of individuals. They aren't to be trusted nor engaged in to have a meeting of the mind.

45.) Some people call you stating that they desire to catch up x see how you are doing, only to get in your business.

—It is unfortunate yet it happens- people come out of the blue, coming out of the woodwork to just say "Hello".
Wait what?
"Just saying hello"?
—Why call if we aren't going to engage in meaningful communication x meeting of the

minds?
—They desire to converse for
only but a few moments to
share little yet inquire much
about you.
—Then state that they are "to
busy" to converse on the
regular.
Yet converse with people via
social media that they may or
may not know or will most
likely not see anytime soon.
—A time in humanity when
there are well over a dozen
modes of communication to
choose from.
—Unless they

desire to build with you-
friendship, business or other.
Communication with this
person isn't worth the
moments that can be used to
build with someone you
desire or converse with x one
that really desires to be there.

46.) People can try their
hardest to help yet things still
happen- there is no reason to
get get out of character- it is
this. Do not depend on others-
make sure you are able to do
most anything yourself

—Things happen.
—Make sure you have your
things in order.
—Quiet yourself and understand
this sooner than later- it is on
you.

47. Most people will have nothing to say when you are doing nothing yet talk about you when you do better for your life, then act as if they were always there for you or they talk about you more.

—I know someone that desired to do better for their life by doing various things. When they weren't doing much of nothing, no one had much to say- [to there face that is.]

—When they started making
strides for progression- the
questions crashed often as the
waves to the shore.
Why this x why that?
Wait a tick-
1.) When they weren't doing
much of anything other than
the basics of human behavior x
life-
they said nothing.
2.) Now they desire x are doing
things to embrace
More Life-
they have words x opinions?
—The other facet is that when
they succeed, they will

110

either act as if they were
always there for them or they
will do as they were doing
before- silent or speaking yet
saying things that aren't to
their face.
—There are many real life
examples that confirm
scenarios as this.
—Keep your peace and
celebrate your progression x
success with those that truly
desire growth x the best for
you in all facets.

48.) <u>People will blame you</u> for something that they decided not do yet it <u>has nothing</u> to do <u>with you.</u> For you are not the reason they did not do it.

—Something they desired to do- they won't do it yet they will blame you for them not achieving that which they desired to do x be.
—When one truly wants to do something- at least in the free world.

Nothing can get in their way
of obtainment x
achievement.
Most times people desire a
punching bag x something
to blame for them not doing
that which they set out to
do.
If they wanted to do it so
strongly- what is stopping
them from doing said things
right now at this moment?
—Never feed into such
claims-

49.) Some are there until it matters

—There while all is
well x prosperous-
yet when a bump comes
jump ship.
—They are those that you
should not place much
stock nor real estate in- in
terms of your feelings, life
or energy.

50.) Some will start the plane with you yet jump out while in the air, not being there to land the plane. In a way, that can be good- for it will force you to stand x rise to the occasion

—One can view this as a bad thing and true it would be preferable to end victorious with the same people that you started with yet at times, that is not

always the case.
—Find the beauty within
that- it allows you to stand
on your own two feet,
conquering that which must
be done.
—Allowing you to
understand that with or
without them, you will
achieve x bring to fruition
all that you set out to do!
—Thank them- keep your
peace and communication
within yourself- of the
beauty x bliss.

51.) People will say that they would do it yet turn around and not do it.

—"If I were you- I would have done this or that"
—Don't take heed to the hype- they say it at times to watch you do it- it could possibly be even for their personal amusement x to speak about you.

52.) No matter how much thought x reason you give someone, they may still keep their mind made up even if it isn't the best.

—Why waste your precious wisdom x insight or try to share x explain your piece to a individual that made up their mind in the beginning of the conversation or even before you started conversing.

—Honestly- unless they are willing to fully hear and analyze your piece [then state Yay x Nay]- say not a word to them. Reciprocity should be had- both of you listening to each others point of view yet their mind was made up to from the beginning.

53.) People go off of first impressions- give them nothing.

—The phrase most have heard- "Make x try to make a good impression"
—Yet when one thinks about it- it's a fairly naive x a unwise concept x thought process.
—How many people have you met that appeared one way [at first impression] yet turned out to be so totally x drastically different?

Many wear mask-
1.) They are afraid of
themselves.
2.) They don't really like
themselves
3.) They were taught to do such
things- whether verbally or
nonverbally
4.) They want to appear a
certain way.
—Be wise and never go off of a
first impression- never fool
yourself.
—People have no choice but to
reveal themselves x their fruit,
inner world.
Commune x obverse in silence.

121

54.) Most people have no code, standard, whatever one would be fond of calling it.

—When one has no form of self integrity- they have no self honor.
—If one has no self honor- their words mean nothing
—They dilute themselves for not only can their word not be trusted for their own inner world x outer life- it most definitely can not be trusted in any

capacity in term of receiving
it for your own application
towards life.
—Limit communication

—

55.) No matter that which
you say- some will always
have something not positive x
productive to say to that
which you state.

Why tell them anything?
Keep it to yourself and
prosper in all facets.

56.) Most people want a rise out of you

—Individuals as this
Never- not ever do you give them an ounce of your energy, time- give them nothing!
For that is chaos x a living hell to dwell in the mist of one that has a mission to disrupt your peace because of the hell which dwells within them.
Their personal discombobulation is not something you have to

124

entertain- it is wise to not have communication with those that desire nothing good for you.
Peace be with you- shut your mouth and live!

—

57.) Most people are passive aggressive

—In the word form they are being sarcastic x underhanded
—In life- doing things that have grounds to be spoken on yet when you desire

to speak- they state that they didn't do anything- that you are the issue. Keep your words and say nothing- converse with those that want something to come out of the conversation- even if the conversation is uncomfortable- for just because it may be uncomfortable, doesn't mean that is should not be spoken on.

58.) Most people want you at the say level they are

—The moment you state I am content yet I desire more- at times you'll find that they have issues with that- yet it is most of the time jealousy x insecurity on their part. For one should celebrate x be inspired to see someone they know x anyone period, prosper in various facets.

59.) Most people do not like different

—Foreign thoughts x idea
—Foreign people
—Foreign experiences
Living that same day over
and over for fear of different.
Different is good- different is
that which allows us all to
learn something new.
If I knew exactly everything
you knew x thought the same
exact way. Would we learn
anything from one another?

Of course not at all-
Difference is beautiful.
Different- Hue, Shapes,
Voices, Sizes, Thoughts,
Ways of doing or looking
at x about something and
the list goes on.
Different is good.
It is more than okay x
grand to be different.
Embrace x share you
difference.

60.) Most people don't know
that success is dependent
upon oneself-

—The perception, of that
which they desire for it to
be.
Not that which another-
school , person, parents,
friends x television- no.
For some, it is waking up x
others it is billions of
dollars x graduating x
making a impact x this x
that

61.) Most people are trying to keep up with someone else- impress another

—That is a mundane thought process.
Love yourself x never get trapped in that- limit communication.
For those that associate with one another influence each other.

—

62.) Most people are okay with going with the status quo

—Tail never he head
Followers

Thinking that there is only one way in life- that most have to follow this way.
They were mentally beaten x embarrass to submission.
—This thinking x way of living is toxic, for it is far from conducive to fully living.
Live- never conform.

63.) Most people think their opinion is God bound

—As written before- as I will write now.
I heard this phrase-
"Opinions are like assholes-
everyone has one"
—Let them think as they will- do not debate.
For what will it breed?
Only chaos within your own soul.
Shut your mouth and let it be.

64.) Most people talk big x bad yet are insecure

-As a little chihuahua - big x bad yet confront them and watch them act as if a tail is between their legs.
—Most of their attacks come from a deep insecurity and that is the only way they feel that they have some form of control x they should act this way- for it is a defense trait.

65.) Most people wear a mask- faux face x smile x life x emotions x words

—How can you trust one that lies to themselves and lies to your face from the first moment you meet them?
—It wouldn't be wise to do so.
—The mask they wear stem from a few things-
1.) It was taught
2.) The aren't secure in whom they are enough within

themselves.
3.) They don't like the real
them.
4.) They know that you
wouldn't like the real them.
The list goes on- the fact of the
matter is- it is not wise to
associate with such individuals
for they aren't whom you
believe them to be nor that
which they portray and they
more than likely don't know
whom they are.
—Their pain is that which they
emulate.
—Doing things for reason that
they do not know why.
—Doing thing to

appease people that they don't really know nor do the people care much for them.
—Living a life that they truly do not desire to life yet place on the mask when they step out never to be viewed as they actually are- more of the way they are fond of being viewed.
—Lying to themselves day after day in order to cope.
—Knowing that they are different yet constantly choosing to blend x hide their true self away.

66.) Most people get mad x afraid when one is able to do that which they aren't

—People often don't like to see that they are not moving forward- living a mundane existence. Knowing that they can do more yet choose not to do more- then regret all the time x moments of the infinite that they have wasted. When they see youunspoken thoughts arise as "Why are they

able to travel, pay for their child's school, create their business, do this, go there, be that."
It's awakens an anger mixed with a fear of being left out, being left behind.
—In a world, that there are some that aren't free.
Yet these individuals are- they chose to be where they are by the actions they have sown- now they reap that which they do not desire. When they had freedom- in the same capacity as you to do that

which they truly desired, if
they practice a bit of
clairvoyance.
Be free- gently walk away
and reap the beauty that
which you have sown.
Yet to continue to plant
seeds, of all that is good.

67.) Most people don't say that with a they mean

—Then the believe that you are do the same as them- placing their limits onto you. Thinking that you also don't mean that which you say. —Communicating with them that choose not to express themselves fully- speaking in code or simply speaking in a way that they do not mean. —That is a waste- shut your mouth and move on.

141

68.) Most people are afraid to be alone- silence

—They only converse for they desire not to be alone with their personal thoughts.
—Question- communicate with one that uses you as a crutch- not for the sake of they genuinely enjoy you? I think not- shut your mouth.
Now if they need help and they enjoy you that is different.

69.) Most people like the idea of something more than actually doing it- example let's say one likes the idea of being a humanitarian, until it is time to do that which a humanitarian does

—Those are the worst- the reason being- they get just as excited, amped, pumped, enthusiastic as you- yet when it comes down to the nitty gritty, they are nowhere to be found.

—You believe their words, believe that you can build with them- that you found one that is ready to shake the world in a grand capacity- for the reality to be that they only enjoyed the idea more than the actual thing.
—There are many as this on our Earth- when you find them, do not place much real estate in them, for you do not desire to waste the most precious things there is to our human shelve life.

[Time]

Most people talk the talk, don't walk the walk
though it is fine to talk the talk as long as you walk the walk at the same time yet never only just talking the talk
—They say talk is cheap yet I stated- let's analyze that statement.

1.) There are many people that earn quite a bit of money from the words that come from their mouth.
—Hmm- so that statement is flawed.

Alright- talk is not cheap yet it is worthless when no actions, execution x bring to fruition is

added the to mix.
Yes talk the talk if you
choose!
Yes be excited about that
which you are about to
create, do or be!
Yet always walk the walk.
Walk the walk over talking
the talk-
Though you can do both.
—Those that just talk placing
no power- action behind their
words that they chose to
conceive and share out of
their mouth.
Stay away from them.

70.) Most people have let life beat them down x tell whom they are

—They have been talked about x bullied.
It is quite unfortunate.
Never allow anyone to beat you down in any capacity nor facet.
Also if you ever see someone bullying another, you must help or get help for the individual.
Yes this is about ["How I Learned to Shut the Fuck Up"]
Yet never ever not once stay silent when seeing something as that.

Uplift your fellow human!
It's more than worth it!
Never allow anyone to tell you
who you are-
You tell you.
You are you.
They aren't you.
They cannot decide that for you.
Stand up for yourself.
Arise!
And if anyone tries to tell you
whom you are-
Give them no words.
Keep your peace x energy and
remove yourself.
Live well- always.
Love Yourself- always

71.) Most people are judgmental

—They never understand the
facets of humans.
That mistakes are life- yet are
they really mistakes?
More as learned experiences-
for how many times did you
stumble while learning to
walk?
Misspoke x mispronounced
while trying to say "Mama x
Dada"?
[Humans are a combination
of experiences x biological
development.]

149

There was never a manual
to the various facets of life-
all are experiencing this
journey, throughout it there
is a possibility that they will
morph quite a bit- that is
fine.
Whether it is on page 1 or
page 50 plus of ones life- it
isn't over, until it is over.
Yet even then- life is life.
People that judge- it would
be wise of them to
understand that, there have
been many living and those
that have

lived x died- that have
changed their life around in
absolutely phenomenal ways.
Also that they- the judger
have traits that can be viewed
this x that way themselves-
so the judger shouldn't judge.
It's quite hypocritical.
Be gentle- yet save your
words with individuals as
that- for to judge is as a "God
complex" and for them that
one judges-
It is as this [Who are you?
What authority do you have
over me?

You are are not
my God nor are you me!]
Most people judge you off of
appearance, no matter how
beautiful your mind or
charter x inner world is
—I am not stating buy clothes
and do things to cause you to
seem more aesthetically
pleasing- far from it.
Nor am I saying go out and
look just anyway.
I'm stating simply- love
yourself.
Clothes don't make you- you
make clothes.
Bump trends-

embrace style!
—Style is determined by
oneself- your unique
outlook on taste x attire.
Those that accept you-
cherish.
Those that don't-
understand that is their
prerogative.
Not all will accept you-
that's more than fine.
Converse with those that
do.
Forget those that don't.
Live.

72.) Most don't have a thirst for knowledge x new frontiers

—Day after day the same- is the name of their game.
— Understand am not speaking on practice- having to do the same things over and over [repetition].
That which I am speaking on is this- those that do not desire to learn, to explore themselves nor life- gaining a new

form of understanding, thinking- viewing themselves x life with new eyes, looking to broaden their horizons.

–

73.) Some people talk because they were taught that was the polite thing to do- not because they desire to converse with you.

—I recently read that someone was invited somewhere yet the didn't want to go because they

spend a year being
a "fake", conversing when
they really didn't feel like it.
The people inviting them
somewhere desired to gain
a connection yet the other
individual would rather
write to a pool of social
media- expressing to many
they hardly have any real
communication with.
Yet that is their
prerogative- their right.

74.) Most ask how are you almost as a nervous tick

—They truly don't care and if you were tell them "how you are" they view you as crazy x weird.
They do it as a formality- feeling a certain way if they don't do it, for it was hard wire in into their core from a young age.
Yet when they do- do it, there is nothing real, no substance, no

feeling- no care.
It is as it would have been
better if they said nothing
at all.
—Since they care none-
give they none of your
words.

—

75.) Most people Let
others define whom they
are

—No identity

76.) Most people allow certain things to determine x ruin their day.

—They allow external things x people to determine their mood x feelings, thoughts, actions x gestures.
Instead of taking control of their being x inner world-facets of them are flung all over the place by outside factors.
—People as that aren't the best communicators, they are only

feeling lead- without the taming of emotions as they see fit.

They aren't the ones that control their feelings x they weren't taught nor took it upon themselves to learn to effectively express their feeling, for emotions are good- when expressed effectively x wisely.

–

77.) Most people don't like themselves and may not like you

—It is more as a-

how can one enjoy you, if they don't enjoy x aren't fond of themselves?
—For one to not enjoy themselves that is something deeply rooted that.
It would be wise for them the to do that which I call x coin as mental clean, inner world cleaning.
—For them to understand where their personal dislike stems from- finding the root and uprooting for it to never sprout again.

78.) Most people are selfish

—There is a world of difference between self love x self confident [that which I greatly enjoy x are fond of] and one being selfish. Thinking only about themselves- many say that they with you yet most likely are not.
—The phrase high x dry was made to perfectly describe these characters.

One moment there- the next,
within the blink of an eye-
gone.
They are individuals that
actions would show, that they
think "loyalty" is and bad
word.
These are those that aren't
the best to communicate
with- in any capacity.
To be great-
to have peace, I do not believe
that one has to be selfish.
People can be whichever way
they desire to be.

Yet when engaging with one
that does not believe in
reciprocity.
It is okay to remove to
yourself from them.
For there is more than
enough for all the gain,
prosper- all that they desire
to be.
[Iron Sharpens Iron]

79.) Most people don't know that the present is a combination of the past- choices x events etc. That the future is the present a combination of "nows". That this moment is the most important of all

—All of the past is the present.
—All of the present is the future.
—That which is done today will in a way will determine your future.
I state [in a way] you must factor in the variables of life.

80.) Most don't feel the moment this second

—Humans have something
that I call a coin as:
[Shelve Life]
That is- we are all given a
body that has the potential
lifespan of conception to
115-120 years.
I say all this to say-
Time is Precious
Time is Limited.
There is noting to fret- it's
life.
Yet while we are alive and
among the many, many

things we can do in the "Play Ground" x gift we call life. That is- feel the moment- understanding that it has passed.
For [Time] is as trying to catch water x sand with ones- one barehand.
Embrace morality- understanding that this is not a television show nor a game.
There are no redo's.
I urge you to feel the moment- now live a life full of appreciation x gratitude.

81.) Most people are afraid to stand up for a just cause.

Big or small.
To their friends x family
Even themselves.
Also things pertaining to our world x fellow humans.

—

82.) Most people would rather nothing be done x built than share

They would rather 100% of nothing
More than they
would 50% of something prosperous.

Yes all have the right to do such things.
Yet why communicate with such individuals that are greedy x not wise- obtaining nothing.
For they practice no wisdom, understand that yes all can do a great some by themselves-
Yet we can do much more together.
Connect with individuals that are [willing] to do everything themselves.
Yet are open to [connection x collaboration.]
Being able to view the beauty in togetherness.

169

83.) Preconceived notion
x Perception of you

—You do little to nothing,
they believe that they
know you.
Because you dressed this
way
You walk that way
Eat this food
Also your skin is that hue.
They have prejudged you-
do not converse with them
to "try" and cause them to
view you

in a different light.
For it is as this- no matter
that which you do- people
will see you in that which
light they see fit.
Yet it doesn't matter what
they think nor that which
they feel about you.

—

84.) People are a puzzle

—Most want to fit-
"belong"
or they are scatter upon
the floor hoping that

someone comes and
places them together- only
they spend time with
those that never finish
puzzles and often never
have all the pieces.
Them not knowing that
are already whole.
To you- it is okay not to fit-
be you x be whole!

85.) People hear every third or fifth word

People think about what they want to say, while they state that they are listening to that which another has to say.
—They do not listen yet speak on that which you spoke as if they did.
Yet by doing so breeds confusion- for if they would have fully listened to every word and not the words

within their head- on that
which they want to say.
There is a possibility that
understanding- if not
agreement that can
blossom to fruition.
-Don't waste precious word
on those that do not honor
your words, energy,
imagination, expression-
and time spent with them
for the sake of communion
x understanding.

86.) Most people won't understand you no matter how much of a picture you paint them

—Some may not understand for their mind may conceive things differently, they aren't at the level mental to receive your thoughts x words or it's cause could be that they purposely choose not to desire to understand.

—In any case- save your voice x precious words- for there are those that will appreciate the grand art that you

are expressing via
the words of your mind x mouth.
Yet to those that think they know
that which one is going to state
before one is able to fully explain
their thought
—That is the worst- for they
engage in communicate to really
not engage.
—It is for the perception that they
are willing to engage.
Not sure if it is to hear themselves
talk or the sense that they desire
to control- among other things.
—I call this the ["Mind Reader
Complex"]- thinking they know
that which is

coming next- to interject their
two cent on the concept x
pathway of thought that you
desired to share with them.
—To find out that you were
about throw that which I coin as
the ["Boomerang Clause"] that
throws them for a loop.
For they saw the boomerang
flying out and said within- "I see
where this is heading" only for
the boomerang to come back
full circle to you- connecting x
tying together all that you
stated x your concept.

91.) Most people have
nothing to say even if they
speak for an hour or two

—No substance, nor passion,
no enthusiasm- nor zest.
They speak about clothes
and television.
Nothing edifying.
For they are not good
communicators x don't
know have to converse.
Yet they do-
Say nothing- Silence is the
best thing to give them.

88.) Most people remember the bad more than they remember the good.

—If you want to be remembered
cause one to [feel]
—Whether good x bad- though it
would be kind to choose good.
—By causing one to feel they
will never forget you- those that
are forgotten rarely stood out,
in most if not all capacities x
cases
—All this being said- it is as this,
though they remember that

you caused them to feel- even
if it was good.
—They mostly remember the
bad- yet that also has to do
with their paradigm of the
mind x character.
—Those that do such things
wouldn't be the best to
communicate with, for even
after something is done and
over with they may still hold
the bad x neglect the good.

89.) Most desire a pawn to keep around, to keep them company or to sacrifice in a moments notice

—

90.) People will blame you for something that they decided not do yet it has nothing to do with you x you are not x were not the reason they did not do it.

—Something they desire to do- they won't do it yet they will blame you for them not achieving that which they

181

desire to do x be.
—When one truly wants to do
something- at least in the free
world.

Nothing can get in their way of
obtainment x achievement.

Most times people desire a
punching bag x something to
blame for them not doing that
which you set out to do.

If they wanted to do it so
strongly- what it stopping them
from doing said things right
now at this moment?

—Never feed into such claims-
limit x stop communication.

91.) Most people take things personally

—Something that may have nothing to do with them they make it about them.
—You may not have even known that which you stated had pertained them in any capacity. Yes I will state that all are going through something- with that being said be gentle with your words.
Though you x all should be able to speaking freely- while being civil in a human to human manner x capacity.

92.) People will tell you that which you x someone else should have done.

—If it is- unsolicited advice x opinions, disregard fully unless that which they are stating has wisdom, truth, something that connects with you.
—If not- what do we do with rotten food?
—Do that with that which they have to say.
For some want to be right no matter if they are wrong or if another way is provided
—At times it can be a lack of control in other areas of their

184

life- them feeling x
unconsciously thinking that
this is the only way that they
have control or this may be
the only thing that they think
they have control in some
form.
—Not worth the energy by
any means-
Though in term of opinion x
perception- a lot of times
there is not [right nor
wrong].
—Only understanding x point
of view.

94.) Some people just want to hear themselves speak

— ...no words.
they talk out of the side
of their neck- speaking
about things they know
little nor nothing about.
—It is more than okay to
not know something- for
you don't know only
until you do

186

know.
—For but in a moment you
can learn.
—Now you know- yet if one
does not know, it is more
than okay with keeping
ones mouth shut and
learning something new.
Yet to those that desire to
not make sense, don't take
the time to sense, don't
know that they don't
make sense
They don't

refine nor edit
themselves-
Thinking about that which
they thought.
Holding it up to
themselves, viewing the
sides of it as if they were
to hear someone else say
that which they just said-
how would they think
about it.
How would they make the
thought more beautiful.

95.) Most people are ego lead

—Ego it toxic.
—Ego is that which causes one to neglect the beauty for the sake of stoking itself.
Ego should never be confused with self love x self confidence.
—Avoid
Also those want to be the smartest person in the room
—Let them [think as they will- stay silent.
Learned from them on which not

to do.
As well as from those that
do not read
—Reading is important-
expands the mind.
—Exposes it to a universe x
pool of thought other than
their own.
—It's gets the gear turning
in a capacity that allows
one to create their own
original thought x concept.
Lastly those that think
correction done in kindness
is mean- no thats their ego.

96.) Most think the timidity is humility

—Timidity is far from Humility.
—Humility is Strength.
—Timidity is a form x trait of weakness.
It is more than okay to have Power, Self Love, Self Confidence.
People may think that you are bragging
When all you are doing it stating facts
Speaking about the only thing that most can be a master of x expert

at- oneself.
It is okay to feel good about
yourself as well and express
such things.
At times some confuse
confidence x self love with
arrogance x conceitedness.
Yet I state that they are a
universe apart-
For one that confuses the two
I would state that they do not
know nor embody neither
confidence nor self love or
they have a false view x
perception of such things of
power.

97.) Most people desire to use your words against you, are fond of labels for concepts are to high for their thoughts

—To say to you- no because you said this or that, while knowing that you meant something entirely different or you say a concept they don't get it.
Yet you say a "label"- for the sake of them- that they may understand, they stay stuck on the one label you said.
Yet the concept is vast and can be a

multitude of things.
There are some that you would
believe have your best interest
yet that is far from the truth
—Not giving you a chance to
fully express that which you
yourself wanted say, that way
you two can have a productive
conversation of understanding
and peace- whether you two
were in agreement or not.
For your peace and theirs-
silence is best.

—

98.) Most people are fickle
—No form of honor, they also
make excuses.

194

99.) Most people lie quite often

—No need to communicate with
a liar
—They do it to should a degree,
that it has now become apart of
them now.
As well as they do it in a
capacity in that which that
leaves them a way out- to state
that "they didn't really lie"

—

100.) Most people have wicked imaginations

—When one conceives what you
did or said in a

certain capacity in that your
you did not do nor would mean.
—That comes from their
personal wick imaginations.
—Something happens and their
first response is that you did
something negative.
—It is best to not communicate
with someone as this.

—

101.) Most people have a heart
beat yet aren't living-
More as a living suicide, living
for they are alive yet living a life
they despise

They aren't willing to do that
which it

takes to fully, truly live life, be
their best self.
Dying inside each day.

—

102.)People will ask you to do
something then curse you for
being diligent in helping them
achieve the endeavor that they
ask for help in fruition of it's
accomplishment.

103.) Goes with number six in the capacity that most are coming from a place from which they were exposed to, experienced, did themselves, observed in life, watched on television or conceived within their inner world.

—That being said- that which they do to you has nothing to to do with you
—Don't take it personally
—Some have not taken responsibility for themselves- editing that which they think x was exposed to in a

multitude of facet in life.
That which is inside has no choice
but to come out.
— For most always reveal
themselves so their is no reason to
pry
—Enjoy the moment and the
individual- things most always
have a way of coming to light.
allowing the results to freely come
to you.

—They show their fruits.
To you- those that are dancing
through life in a capacity in that
which you do not desire to dance.
Shut your mouth and enjoy your
on rhythm.

199

104.) People will tell you that
you can't do it

—Yet if you tell them
nothing- they say nothing.
—It is better to be an
announcer of done
endeavors that way all that
they have to say is "oh"
—For if you tell them
beforehand most aren't
going to tell you anything
worth hearing.
—Say nothing.

105.) People will say they don't like it

—Yet will turn around and do it- not giving any credit, basically "plagiarizing" all that you confided with them.
—Tell them nothing!

—

106.) People will mock you

—What would be the reason to communicate with one that does such things- whether they agree x disagree all can converse in a manner that is suitable for all parties x individuals involved. Yes they can do as they please yet you do not have to subject yourself you should toxic traits.

107.) Most want to be understood yet one should not if they must comprise themselves

—

108.) It is this- if it is good x honoring the life x rights of our fellow humans.

—Stand up for that which you believe in
Yet I will say choose your words as well as your "battles"
Words have a

place indeed- yet
action!
Action breed results

—

109.) Most people treasure
things x not people
People are the most important.

—Things may be replaced-
people can not.
Each life is it's own and unique
there is no other them.
Treasure your loved ones.
Called them, go see them-
embrace them.
People are far, far, far more
valuable than things.

204

110.) People will give input based off of what they are fond of not based off of that with is better for you.

—It is as this- you ask someone "Which color looks good on me? Blue, Red, Orange, Black or Purple"
—Most will say that "they like Orange so you should wear Orange."
Yet that is not which you asked- for you are saying, if Black or Purple looks best on you at the moment,

that is what you desire for
them to divulge.
Not their favorite color or
that which they would wear-
for that it not which you
asked.
—Shut your mouth and not
ask- even if you do that wont
really answer the question.

—

111.) Most don't know nor
accept development x
experience
That one can learn all things-
choosing that which they
learn x

continue
As a baby- did you know
how to talk x walk?
Were you the height that
you are now?
Yet you learned x you
developed.
All of that trial and error.
Stumbling physically in
learning to walk x
verbally in words.

112.) Most people may view this as fluff

Yet it is far from it.
It is things that most have
faced a number of times.
This is needed- indeed.
For that which not to do- as
all as that which to up root
if it is found within one that
reads or hear of this which I
have composed.
If one has something other
that beautiful to stated
about this

writing- I have nothing to say to you.
Yes I can think of things to say as all can.
Yet I desire to not engage in that which you have to say.
To those that are fond of that which I have composed.
Gratitude!
I appreciated it.
Either way whether one is for or the opposite for me.
Thank you-
Power to you all.
Love yourself.
Prosper in all facets- always.

113.) Most people will call you weird

Only for the sake of doing
something different
Be different
Be weird
By all means-
Be YOU.

You don't have to be friends
with everyone-
Not everyone has to be your
friend,
Not everyone will be your
friend,
That is fine.
Just because you are friends
with someone- doesn't mean
that you have to be friend with
their friends
Not everyone will love you x
accept you- that is fine. Though
put out love anyway- yet never
allow yourself to be anyones
punching bag- not even by

yourself.
When you control yourself-
your thoughts x emotion-
No one will be able to control
you.
For if one can cause you to act a
certain way- they control you.
Choose your thoughts x
emotions
Choose your words x when not
to speak.
Be mindful whom you surround
yourself with-
Give thought x energy too
Do not allow everyone in- be
civil x kind yet not

everyone is for you.
Understanding that some are
around for but a moment
while others- a life time.

In a interconnected world-
there are so many facets to the
inner world of the multitude of
humans each of us will have to
come in contact with during our
life time.
Instead of trying to be accepted
and or trying to persuade or
convince others why you should
be loved- one should know x
understand their self worth.
Having self love x self
confidence-
coming to terms

that not everyone will love nor accept you.
Though that is more than fine- for there are many that will cherish you for that which you are and that which to are morphing to become.
A piece written on and about the human condition [Anthropology x Psychology] - that which one may face or do and how to have peace in the mist of it all or personal acknowledgment- that said individual can up root. Knowing that they

a capable of doing all which
they desire- while honoring the
life x rights of all and a
reminder or telling they have a
choice in all facets of life-
[Health, Wealth, Love,
Happiness] internal and out.
A reflection
An acknowledgment that no life
isn't a fairytale yet that one's
life x the life of humanity can be
made better- yet it starts one
person at a time x in daily civil
human to human interaction.

-Armand Cook

Be gentle with one another for all exhibit various traits at various times in this thing we know as life.

Be gentle yet diligent, responsible, accountable with yourself.

How I Learned to Shut the Fuck Up

How I Learned to Shut the Fuck Up

By: Armand Cook

Thursday, November 1, 2018
11:40 PM

ArmandCook.com
PostalMontage.com
HowILearnedToShutTheFuckUp.com

@HowILearnedToShutTheFuckUp

HowILearnedToShutUp@gmail.com

Made in the USA
Monee, IL
14 July 2023